WHY DOES FOOD GO BAD?

By Benjamin Proudfit

Gareth Stevens
PUBLISHING

Please visit our website, www.garethstevens.com. For a free color catalog of all our high-quality books, call toll free 1-800-542-2595 or fax 1-877-542-2596.

Library of Congress Cataloging-in-Publication Data

Proudfit, Benjamin, author.
 Why does food go bad? / Benjamin Proudfit.
    pages cm. — (Everyday mysteries)
 ISBN 978-1-4824-3848-2 (pbk.)
 ISBN 978-1-4824-3849-9 (6 pack)
 ISBN 978-1-4824-3850-5 (library binding)
 1. Food spoilage—Juvenile literature. 2. Food—Microbiology—Juvenile literature. 3.
 Food—Preservation—Juvenile literature. I. Title. II. Series: Everyday mysteries.
 QR201.F62P76 2016
 664.001'579—dc23

                            2015031496

Published in 2016 by
Gareth Stevens Publishing
111 East 14th Street, Suite 349
New York, NY 10003

Copyright © 2016 Gareth Stevens Publishing

Designer: Katelyn E. Reynolds
Editor: Kristen Nelson

Photo credits: Cover, p. 1 Irina Mos/Shutterstock.com; pp. 3–24 (background) Natutik/Shutterstock.com; p. 5 Voyagerix/Shutterstock.com; p. 7 Tibanna79/ Shutterstock.com; p. 9 06photo/Shutterstock.com; p. 11 (inset) Science Picture Co/Collection Mix: Subjects/Getty Images; p. 11 (main) NorGal/Shutterstock.com; p. 13 Ekaterina_Minaeva/Shutterstock.com; p. 15 E R DEGGINGER/Science Source/ Getty Images; p. 17 Forewer/Shutterstock.com; p. 19 mubus7/Shutterstock.com; p. 21 Macrovector/Shutterstock.com.

Printed in the United States of America

CPSIA compliance information: Batch #CW16GS: For further information contact Gareth Stevens, New York, New York at 1-800-542-2595.

CONTENTS

Boldface words appear in the glossary.

Don't Eat That!

It's unpleasant to bite into a soft apple or have a sandwich made with stale bread. Many foods can stay fresh for a long time when kept cool and dry. But almost everything goes bad sometime!

We often say food has "gone bad" when it's no longer the **consistency** or taste we expect. These changes mean the food has begun to break down, or decay. They also mean the food could make you sick.

Fruits and Veggies

Once a fruit or vegetable is picked, it starts to decay. The fruits and vegetables at the grocery store have been stored at cool **temperatures** to make this happen more slowly. Higher temperatures cause faster decay.

Microorganisms, such as bacteria, cause the breakdown of fruits and vegetables. Because these foods are made of mostly water, microorganisms like to grow on them. In addition to warmth, **moistness** helps them grow more quickly.

listeria

11

The Bad Spot

You can tell a fruit or vegetable has gone bad when it starts to have spots that are the wrong color. They may grow fuzzy **mold** or get soft. When left to decay too long, some fruits and veggies will smell!

13

Spoiled Meat

Microorganisms cause raw meat to go bad, or spoil, too. Some bacteria in meat may have already been there when the animal was alive. If allowed to grow too much, these bacteria can make the meat unsafe for people to eat.

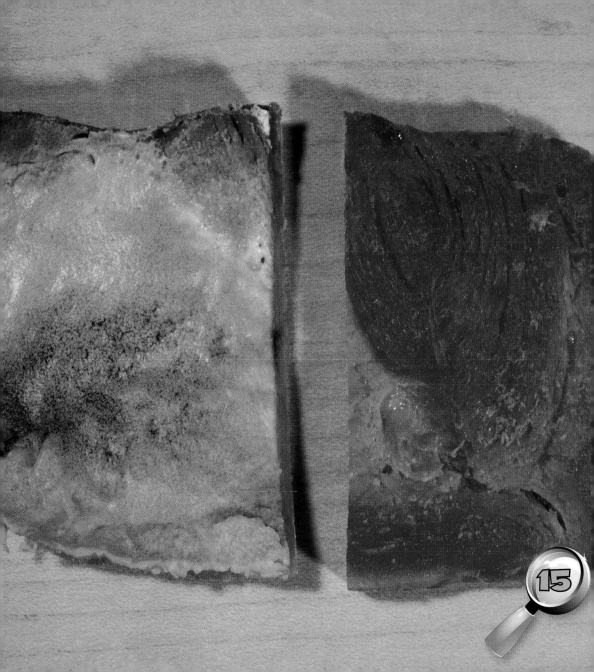

That Stinks!

It's often easy to tell if meat is spoiled. It will smell really bad and start to change color. Cooking at a high enough temperature kills a lot of bacteria. However, if raw meat is spoiled, no cooking can save it.

Dry Bread

Bread has a lot of starch in it, which is a kind of sugar. At certain temperatures, the starch forms tiny crystals that dry out bread. Bacteria in the air can make bread stale, too! Bread can also grow mold.

Preservatives

Some foods have preservatives added to them to keep them fresh longer. Preservatives are **chemicals** that stop bacteria from growing and other decay from happening. However, eating too many of some preservatives in food can harm your health.

KEEP FOOD FRESH!

storing fruits and vegetables

- wash, but dry before storing
- keep most below 40°F (4.4°C)
- some—such as bananas, lemons, and potatoes—can be kept at room temperature or cooler

storing raw meat

- can be kept frozen
- keep below 40°F (4.4°C) when unfrozen
- check foodsafety.gov for how long each kind of meat can be kept unfrozen

storing bread

- keep in a sealed **container**
- keep away from light and heat
- store at room temperature

21

GLOSSARY

chemical: matter that can be mixed with other matter to cause changes

consistency: how firm, soft, or tough something is

container: an object that can hold something

microorganism: a tiny living thing such as bacteria, mold, or yeast

moistness: wetness

mold: a kind of fungus, or a living thing that is somewhat like a plant, but doesn't make its own food, have leaves, or have a green color

temperature: how hot or cold something is

FOR MORE INFORMATION

BOOKS

Leet, Karen M. *Food Intruders: Invisible Creatures Lurking in Your Food.* Mankato, MN: Capstone Press, 2012.

Rice, Dona Herweck. *Always Growing: Fruit.* Huntington Beach, CA: Teacher Created Materials, 2016.

WEBSITES

Food Safety Game
www.fsis.usda.gov/Oa/foodsafetymobile/mobilegame.swf
Learn more about food safety by playing this game.

Why Does Food Decay?
science-sparks.com/2012/03/05/rotting-apples
Ask an adult to help you do this activity to see how an apple can rot over time.

Publisher's note to educators and parents: Our editors have carefully reviewed these websites to ensure that they are suitable for students. Many websites change frequently, however, and we cannot guarantee that a site's future contents will continue to meet our high standards of quality and educational value. Be advised that students should be closely supervised whenever they access the Internet.

INDEX